PRESERVES

An Hachette UK Company
www.hachette.co.uk

First published in Great Britain in 2012
by Hamlyn
a division of Octopus Publishing Group
Endeavour House
189 Shaftesbury Avenue
London WC2H 8JY
www.octopusbooks.co.uk

Some of these recipes have previously
appeared in other books published by
Hamlyn.

ISBN: 978-0-600-62521-6

A CIP catalogue record for this book is
available from the British Library

Printed and bound in China

10 9 8 7 6 5 4 3 2 1

Both metric and imperial measurements are given in all recipes.
Use one set of measurements, not a mixture of both.

Standard level spoon measurements are used in all recipes
1 tablespoon = one 15 ml spoon
1 teaspoon = one 5 ml spoon

Eggs should be medium unless otherwise stated. The
Department of Health advises that eggs should not be
consumed raw. This book contains a recipe made with lightly
cooked eggs. It is prudent for vulnerable people such as
pregnant and nursing mothers, invalids, the elderly, babies and
young children to avoid uncooked or lightly cooked dishes
made with eggs. Once prepared, these dishes should be kept
refrigerated and used promptly.

This book also includes recipes made with nuts. It is advisable
for those with known allergic reactions to nuts and nut
derivatives and those who may be potentially vulnerable to
these allergies, such as pregnant and nursing mothers, invalids,
the elderly, babies and children to avoid dishes made with nuts
and nut oils. It is also prudent to check the labels of pre-prepared
ingredients for the possible inclusion of nut derivatives.

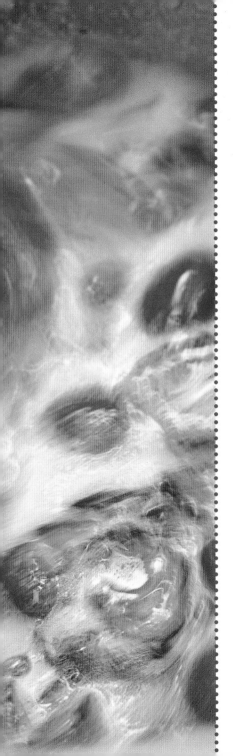

contents

introduction

There is nothing as delicious as homemade preserves and they make great gifts for family and friends too. Here is some essential information to help you to get started.

Basic equipment

Preserving pan
This should be at least 25 cm (10 inches) in diameter and 11 cm (4½ inches) deep. They need to be this wide to allow for good evaporation and to give the contents room to boil without boiling over. As a guide, never fill it more than half full.

Preserving pans are available in aluminium, stainless steel, enamel and copper. Copper pans heat up quickly but are unsuitable for making chutney as the vinegar in chutney reacts with the metal. Whichever you choose, make sure it has a thick base as this reduces the chances of your jam or chutney burning.

Sugar thermometer
Using a sugar thermometer makes it easy to judge when jams and jellies are coming up to set.

Jelly bag
Straining fruit through a bag is essential when making jellies to ensure crystal clear juice. The finer the mesh of the cloth of the jelly bag, the finer the finished jelly will be.

First suspend the bag from a specially designed frame or by tying string to the loops and suspending it from an upturned stool or eye-level cupboard handle. Scald a large bowl with boiling water, empty it, then place it beneath the bag so the bottom of the bag is just above the bowl. Fill the bag with the cooked fruit and cooking liquid and leave undisturbed fro 3–4 hours or overnight so that juice can run out into the bowl. Avoid squeezing the bag or the juice will go cloudy.

After use, wash the bag well in boiling water – don't use detergent or washing-up liquid – and dry thoroughly before stirring.

Spoons

Use a long-handled wooden spoon for stirring, to keep your hand away from the hot preserve. At the end of cooking, remove any scum with a flat stainless steel perforated spoon with small holes.

Jam funnel

Made of metal to withstand the heat of just-cooked preserves, a jam funnel reduces spills down the sides of jars and helps to eliminate scalds when potting preserves.

Jars, bottles and tops

Recycle jam jars for jams, jellies, marmalades, fruit butters and chutneys.

Bottling fruit requires purpose-bought bottling jars with rubber rings or gaskets and spring or screw lids. The most commonly sold are glass Le Parfait jars with metal spring clasps and orange rings. They are widely available and come in a variety of sizes.

Check all jars carefully before use and throw away any with cracks or chips. Soak the rubber rings of Le Parfait jars in warm water for 5–10 minutes before use so that they fit snugly on to the top of the jar.

The importance of sterilizing

Hygiene is really important when preserving and especially when potting the finished preserves. Make sure jars are well washed, rinsed with hot water and dried, then sterilized in a warm oven for 10 minutes. Alternatively jars can be sterilized on a standard wash cycle in a dishwasher and filled while still warm if indicated. Ensure they are dry before filling them. You should also sterilize jam funnels and screw-topped lids.

Covering preserves

How you cover the finished preserve is crucial. For jams, jellies, marmalades and chutneys, always press a disc of waxed paper (available in packs with cellophane jam pot covers and labels), waxed side down, on to the surface of the preserve while it is still very hot. Add a cellophane cover and secure with a rubber band or add a sterilized screw-topped lid and leave to cool. As the preserve cools, the heat kills any bacteria or mildew spores from the air trapped between the lid and the waxed disc.

Chutneys, which also require a waxed disc, and pickles must also have a good, plastic-coated airtight lid – not just to keep the bacteria out but to stop the vinegar evaporating.

If the preserve has to stand for fruit to settle before potting then it is best, after adding the waxed disc, to wait until the preserve is cold before sealing.

Label each jar to identify its contents and add the date when it was made.

Storage

The key to successful and long storage of preserves is a cool, dark place away from direct sunlight. Refrigerate preserves after opening.

How to make perfect preserves

Choosing the fruit
Choose fruit that is firm and ripe or just under-ripe. Cut out any blemishes, then weigh the fruit. Depending on the type of fruit, either rinse with water and pat dry with kitchen paper or wipe clean.

Which sugar is best?
Lump, preserving or granulated sugars are best when making jams, jellies and conserves as they dissolve to a colourless liquid and don't affect the natural colour of the fruit. Preserving sugar dissolves faster than the others and produces less scum, but it is more expensive. Golden granulated or soft light brown sugar may be added to marmalade for a darker, more strongly flavoured finish.

Unless a specific sugar is indicated in the recipe, use lump, preserving or granulated.

Initial cooking
All fruit requires cooking before the sugar is added and timings depend on the fruit used – from 10–15 minutes for delicate berry fruits and up to 45–60 minutes for cooking apples or citrus fruits. The volume of water needed also varies, with more needed for fruit that requires longer cooking times.

Adding sugar
Always warm the sugar before adding it to the hot liquid so that it dissolves quickly. Adding cold sugar will make the temperature of the preserve drop and, by the time it has risen once more, you will be in danger of overcooking the preserve.

What is pectin?
Pectin is a natural, gum-like substance found in varying amounts in the seeds, pips, cores, and skins of fruit. When fruit is crushed and warmed pectin is released and mixes with the natural acids in the fruit to produce a jelly-like set.

Fruits that are low in pectin are often mixed with others that are high in pectin, such as strawberries with red currants and rhubarb and apple. Freshly squeezed lemon juice is often added to strawberry jam and citric acid, available from the chemist, can also be added. Commercially made pectin or preserving sugar with added pectin and citric acid can also be used.

To warm sugar, tip it into a roasting tin and warm for 10 minutes in a preheated oven, 160–180°C (325–350°F), Gas Mark 3–4.

Testing for set

Once the sugar has been added to the cooked fruit and has dissolved, a set should almost be reached within 10–20 minutes of rapid boiling. Longer than that and the preserve will be very dark and overcooked. There are several ways of testing whether a preserve has reached setting point:

Flake test After 10–15 minutes, stir the preserve well with a wooden spoon, then turn the spoon in your hand to cool it a little and allow the preserve to drop from it. If the preserve is ready, it will partly set on the spoon and the drops will fall cleanly off the spoon. If the preserve runs freely off the spoon back into the pan, it is not ready.

Saucer test After 10–15 minutes, turn off the heat, then spoon a little of the preserve on to a saucer. Put it into the freezer for 2–3 minutes, then run a finger through the preserve. If it wrinkles and the indentation made by your finger remains, the preserve is ready. If not, turn the heat back on and continue to boil the fruit, checking at 5-minute intervals, until it reaches setting point.

Using a thermometer Clip a sugar thermometer over the side of the preserving pan when you first begin to cook the preserve so that thermometer and preserve warm up together. As the preserve will be hotter in the centre of the pan, stir well before checking the thermometer. Setting point is 105°C (221°F).

Bottling

To bottle fruit in the oven, following the recipe, pour boiling syrup over cold fruit that has been placed in sterilized jars. Pack each jar carefully. The tighter the fruit is packed into the jar, the less likely the fruit is to rise during heating. Fill the jars to the brim with sugar syrup to allow for the fruit to shrink during cooking. Once filled, tap the jars on the work surface to release any air bubbles or burst air bubbles with a small knife. Loosely screw or fasten the lids so that air can escape.

Then stand the jars on a baking sheet, spaced well apart, and cook in the centre of a preheated oven 150°C (300°F), Gas Mark 2, for 15–40 minutes, depending on the size and firmness of the fruit, or until the fruit just begins to rise in the syrup. Small to medium jars are best for this method and make sure that you leave at least 5 cm (2 inches) between the jars so that the heat can circulate.

At the end of cooking, seal the lids tightly. Check jars the following day to make sure a vacuum has formed. You have a good seal when the lids stay firmly in place even though the metal rings or clasps have been loosened.

This method of bottling is not suitable for fruits that require longer cooking times, such as pears and quinces.

Know your preserves

• Bottled fruit is fruit preserved by soaking it in flavoured sugar syrup or a combination of sugar and alcohol.
• Butters are made from fruit purées cooked with sugar until the consistency of thick cream.
• Conserves are jams with a slightly softer set and are generally made with a mix of whole and crushed fruit.
• Chutneys are a cross between a pickle and a jam with a sweet and sour taste.
• Curds usually contain butter and eggs, in addition to fruit. As they contain eggs, they must be stored in the refrigerator and used within one month.
• Jams are made from crushed fruit and should have a slightly runnier set than jellies.
• Jellies are clear preserves made from cooking diced fruit, with its pips, seeds, skins and cores, in water. It is then strained to make a clear juice and boiled with sugar until set firm.
• Marmalades are jams made exclusively from citrus fruits.
• Mincemeat is made with minced dried fruit and grated or cooked apples and is flavoured with sugar, alcohol and spices. It is traditionally served at Christmas.
• Pickles are made from vegetables or fruit, usually preserved in sweetened vinegar.
• Relishes can be cooked or uncooked and tend to be more spicy than chutneys.

raspberry & redcurrant jam

makes: 1.5 kg (3 lb)
preparation time: 15 minutes
cooking time: about 1 hour

500 g (1 lb) raspberries
500 g (1 lb) redcurrants
300 ml (½ pint) water
juice of 2 lemons
1 kg (2 lb) sugar

1 Mix the fruit in a large pan and add the water. Bring to the boil, then reduce the heat and cover the pan. Simmer for 20–30 minutes, until the redcurrants are really tender.

2 Add the lemon juice and sugar and stir over a low heat until the sugar has completely dissolved.

3 Increase the heat and bring to the boil, then boil hard to setting point. Remove the pan from the heat and, using a slotted spoon, carefully skim off any scum.

4 Transfer the jam to warm dry jars. Cover the surface of each with a disc of waxed paper, waxed side down, then top with an airtight lid or cellophane cover. Label and leave to cool, then store in a cool, dark place. It will keep for 3–4 months.

If you do not like too many seeds in jam, then cook half the fruit separately and press it through a sieve before adding it to the remaining fruit.

pineapple & passion fruit jam

makes: about 2 kg (4 lb)
preparation time: 15 minutes
cooking time: 2½ hours

1 large ripe pineapple
750 g (1½ lb) cooking apples, roughly chopped
6 passion fruit, cut into quarters
1.2 litres (2 pints) water
1.5 kg (3 lb) sugar
juice of 2 large lemons

When properly ripe, passion fruit will have wrinkly skins and feel heavy for their size. Their fragrant pulp combines well with the sweet juicy flesh of the pineapple in this fruity jam.

1 Peel the pineapple and roughly chop the peel together with any leaves. Put the chopped peel and leaves into a pan with the apples and passion fruit and pour in the water. Bring to the boil, then reduce the heat, cover the pan and simmer for 1 hour.

2 Meanwhile, chop the pineapple flesh, cutting up the hard core more finely than the soft part of the fruit.

3 Press the cooked pulp through a fine sieve, pour the resulting purée back into the pan and add the fresh pineapple. Bring the fruit mixture slowly to the boil, then reduce the heat to a simmer, cover the pan and cook the fruit for 30 minutes or until quite tender.

4 Add the sugar and lemon juice and cook over a low heat, stirring continuously, until the sugar has completely dissolved. Bring to the boil and boil hard to setting point. Remove from the heat and, using a slotted spoon, carefully skim off any scum.

5 Transfer the jam to warm dry jars, cover the surface of each with a disc of waxed paper, waxed side down, then top with an airtight lid or cellophane cover. Label and leave to cool, then store in a cool, dark place. It will keep for 3–4 months.

strawberry & champagne conserve

makes: 2.25 kg (5 lb)
preparation time: 10 minutes,
plus standing
cooking time: 20 minutes

1.5 kg (3 lb) strawberries,
hulled
1.5 kg (3 lb) preserving sugar
with added pectin
150 ml (¼ pint) or 1 glass
dry Champagne or
sparkling white wine
1½ teaspoons citric acid

1 Pick over the strawberries and discard any bruised or very soft ones. Halve or quarter them depending on their size, then put half of them into a large pan and roughly crush with a potato masher. If the strawberries are difficult to mash, warm them a little in the pan and then try again.

2 Add the sugar, the remaining strawberries, the Champagne or wine and citric acid and heat gently for 10 minutes, stirring continuously, until the sugar has completely dissolved.

3 Increase the heat and boil rapidly for 5–10 minutes, testing at 5-minute intervals until a set is reached. Using a slotted spoon, carefully skim off any scum, then leave the conserve to stand for 15 minutes to allow the fruit to settle.

4 Transfer the conserve to warm dry jars. Cover the surface of each with a disc of waxed paper, waxed side down, and leave until cold. Top the cold jars with airtight lids or cellophane covers. Label and store in a cool, dark place. It will keep for 6–12 months.

This timeless favourite has been given the star treatment with the addition of Champagne. Serve with thickly sliced bread and butter, warm scones, crumpets or toast.

blackberry & apple jam

makes: about 3.25 kg (7 lb)
preparation time: 15 minutes, plus standing
cooking time: 1 hour

1 kg (2 lb) slightly under-ripe blackberries, stalks discarded
1.75 kg (3½ lb) sugar
1 kg (2 lb) cooking apples
300 ml (½ pint) water
juice of 2 large lemons

Blackberry and apple jam is delicious on hot buttered toast and in jam tarts, or you can pile it lavishly on the base of a custard tart to create a delicious dessert.

1 Layer the blackberries in a large bowl with the sugar and leave to stand overnight.

2 Peel, core and slice the apples. Place all the trimmings in a pan and pour in the water. Bring to the boil and boil, uncovered, for about 20 minutes until most of the water has evaporated and the trimmings are pulpy. Press the mixture through a fine sieve into a large pan.

3 Add the apple slices to the pan and pour in the blackberries with all their juice and any undissolved sugar. Heat the mixture gently to simmering point, stirring continuously, for about 10 minutes until the sugar has completely dissolved and the fruit is soft. Add the lemon juice.

4 Bring the jam to the boil and boil hard to setting point. Remove from the heat and, using a slotted spoon, carefully skim off any scum.

5 Transfer the jam to warm dry jars. Cover the surface of each with a disc of waxed paper, waxed side down, then top with an airtight lid or cellophane cover. Label and leave to cool, then store in a cool, dark place. It will keep for 3–4 months.

gooseberry & almond conserve

makes: about 1.5 kg (3 lb)
preparation time: 15 minutes
cooking time: 1 hour

1 kg (2 lb) gooseberries,
topped and tailed
125 g (4 oz) blanched
almonds, halved
juice of 3 lemons
300 ml (½ pint) water
1 kg (2 lb) sugar

1 Put the gooseberries into a pan with the nuts, lemon juice and water. Bring to the boil, then reduce the heat and cover the pan. Simmer for 20 minutes until the fruit is soft.

2 Add the sugar and cook over a low heat, stirring continuously, until the sugar has completely dissolved. Increase the heat and bring to the boil, then boil, uncovered, for 20 minutes, stirring occasionally, until thickened to a heavy syrup.

3 Transfer the conserve to hot jars and cover the surface of each with a disc of waxed paper, waxed side down, then top with an airtight lid or cellophane cover. Label and leave to cool, then store in a cool, dark place. It will keep for 3–4 months.

The almonds add texture to the gooseberries in this conserve. Serve it as a topping on simple baked apples or as a fruit sauce with apple pies, rice puddings and ice cream.

cherry conserve

makes: about 1.5 kg (3 lb)
preparation time: 15 minutes
cooking time: 1¼ hours

1 kg (2 lb) sour cherries
(Morello or Montmorency),
pitted
1 kg (2 lb) sugar
150 ml (¼ pint) brandy
or orange liqueur
(Cointreau, Curaçao)

1 Put the cherries into a large pan and add the sugar. Pour in the brandy or liqueur and cook over a low heat, stirring continuously, until the sugar has completely dissolved.

2 Bring the fruit to the boil, then lower the heat and simmer gently, uncovered, stirring occasionally, for about 1 hour until it is reduced to about two-thirds of its original volume.

3 Transfer the conserve to warm dry jars. Cover the surface of each with a disc of waxed paper, waxed side down, then top with an airtight lid or cellophane cover. Label and leave to mature in a cool, dark place for about 1 month before using, or store, unopened, for 3–4 months.

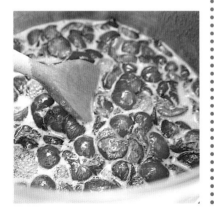

This delicious conserve is perfect as an accompaniment to a special dessert. Use it to fill a sponge flan, top a creamy vanilla mousse or pour into individual semolina moulds.

grape & port jelly

makes: about 1.5 kg (3 lb)
preparation time: 10 minutes
cooking time: 1¾ hours plus
overnight straining

1 kg (2 lb) red grapes with
stalks, halved
3 lemons, halved
1.8 litres (3 pints) water
about 750 g (1½ lb) sugar
150 ml (¼ pint) port

*This is a soft-setting jelly, which
should be stored in a cool place.
It has an excellent flavour and
will complement any home-
made ice cream, vanilla mousse
or delicate cheesecake.*

1 Put the grapes into a large pan with their stalks. Squeeze and reserve the juice from the lemons. Chop the lemon shells and add to the pan with the water. Bring to the boil, reduce the heat and cover the pan. Simmer for 1 hour and allow to cool, then strain the mixture overnight through a jelly bag suspended over a large bowl.

2 The next day, measure the resulting juice and pour it into a large pan. Add 375 g (12 oz) sugar for each 600 ml (1 pint) of juice. Pour in the port and lemon juice and cook over a low heat, stirring continuously, until the sugar has completely dissolved. Increase the heat and bring to the boil, then boil hard to setting point. Using a slotted spoon, carefully skim off any scum.

3 Transfer the jelly to warm dry jars. Cover the surface of each with a disc of waxed paper, waxed side down, then top with an airtight lid or cellophane cover. Label and leave to cool, then store in a cool, dark place. It will keep for 3–4 months.

mint & apple jelly

makes: about 1.5–2 kg (3–4 lb)
preparation time: 30 minutes,
plus straining and standing
cooking time: 1½ hours

2 kg (4 lb) cooking apples,
roughly chopped
300 ml (½ pint) white
vinegar
600 ml (1 pint) water
1.5 kg (3 lb) sugar
125 g (4 oz) stalks of
fresh mint

*This is a traditional way of
preserving mint for use in the
very early spring and winter
months. You can also try using
rosemary instead of mint, or
a selection of mixed herbs.
Serve with roast lamb.*

1 Put the apples into a pan with the vinegar and water. Bring to the boil, then lower the heat and cover the pan. Simmer for 1 hour until the fruit is reduced to a pulp. Allow to cool slightly, then strain the mixture overnight through a jelly bag suspended over a large bowl.

2 The next day, pour the resulting juice into into a large pan and add the sugar. Cook over a low heat, stirring continuously, until the sugar has completely dissolved. Increase the heat and bring to a rapid boil, then boil hard to setting point.

3 Pick the leaves from the mint and chop them finely. Using a slotted spoon, carefully skim off any scum from the jelly, then stir in the mint. Leave to stand for 10 minutes, then stir well and transfer to warm dry jars.

4 Cover the surface of each with a disc of waxed paper, waxed side down, then leave until cold. Top the cold jars with airtight lids or cellophane covers. Label and store in a cool, dark place. It will keep for 3–4 months.

BUTTERS, CURDS, MARMALADES & MINCEMEATS

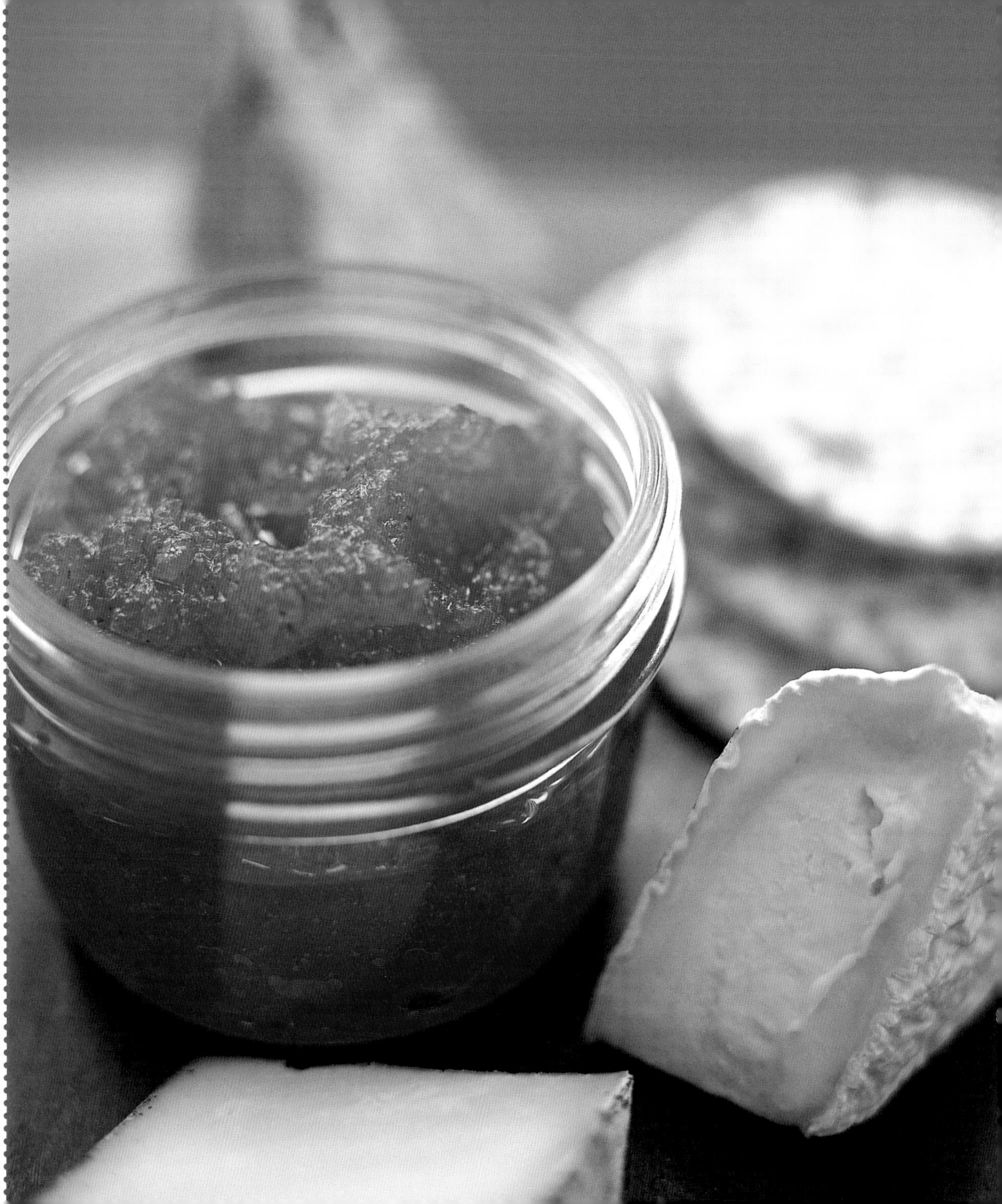

spiced apple butter

makes: about 1.5 kg (3 lb)
preparation time: 20 minutes
cooking time: 1¾ hours

1.25 kg (2½ lb) cooking
apples, roughly chopped
1 cinnamon stick
1 teaspoon freshly
grated nutmeg
1 lemon, chopped
600 ml (1 pint) water
about 625 g (1¼ lb) sugar

1 Put the apples into a pan with the spices, chopped lemon and the water. Bring to the boil, then reduce the heat and cover the pan. Simmer for 1 hour, or until the fruit is reduced to a pulp.

2 Press the mixture through a fine sieve, then weigh the resulting purée and put it into a clean pan. Add 375 g (12 oz) sugar for each 500 g (1 lb) of purée and cook over a low heat, stirring continuously, until the sugar has completely dissolved. Increase the heat and bring to the boil, then boil hard for about 30 minutes, stirring frequently, until the mixture is reduced by half and is thick and creamy.

3 Transfer the butter to warm pots and cover each with a disc of waxed paper, waxed side down, then top with an airtight lid or cellophane cover. Label and leave to cool, then store in a cool dark place for up to 3 months.

Windfall apples are ideal for this preserve. Cut out any bad parts before weighing, but do not bother to peel them as the cooked fruit will be sieved.

lime & passion fruit curd

makes: 650 g (1 lb 5 oz)
preparation time: 15 minutes
cooking time: 30 minutes

250 g (8 oz) caster sugar
juice and grated rind of
4 limes
125 g (4 oz) unsalted butter,
cut into pieces
4 eggs
3 passion fruit

1 Quarter fill a medium pan with water and bring to the boil. Set a large bowl on the pan, making sure that the base is not touching the water. Put the sugar and lime rind into the bowl and press against the edge of the bowl with a wooden spoon to release the oils from the rind.

2 Pour the lime juice into the bowl through a sieve and add the butter. Heat, stirring occasionally, until the butter has melted.

3 Beat the eggs in a separate bowl, then strain into the sugar mixture and stir well. Continue cooking for 20–30 minutes, stirring occasionally, until very thick.

4 Take the bowl off the pan. Halve the passion fruit and, using a teaspoon, scoop the seeds into the lime curd. Mix together gently, then transfer to warm dry jars. Cover each with a disc of waxed paper, waxed side down, then top with an airtight lid or cellophane cover. Label and leave to cool, then store in the refrigerator. It will keep for up to 1 month.

The passion fruit seeds add a wonderful perfume and delicate flavour that's very moreish when spread on warm scones or folded into whipped cream for a wonderfully easy cake filling.

Variations
For lemon curd, use 2½ lemons in place of the limes. For a mixed citrus curd use 1 lemon, 1 orange and 1 lime.

dark orange & lemon marmalade

makes: about 2 kg (4 lb)
preparation time: 30 minutes, plus standing
cooking time: 2 hours

2 large oranges, finely chopped and pips discarded
4 large lemons, finely chopped and pips discarded
1.8 litres (3 pints) water
1 kg (2 lb) sugar
250 g (8 oz) muscovado sugar

1 Put the fruit into a large pan and add the water. Bring to the boil, reduce the heat and cover the pan. Simmer for 1½ hours.

2 Add all the sugar to the pan and cook over a low heat, stirring continuously, until the sugar has completely dissolved. Increase the heat and bring to a rolling boil, then boil hard to setting point. Using a slotted spoon, carefully skim off any scum, then leave the marmalade to stand for 15 minutes to allow the fruit to settle.

3 Stir the marmalade, then transfer to warm dry jars. Cover the surface of each with a disc of waxed paper, waxed side down, then leave until cold. Top the cold jars with airtight lids or cellophane covers. Label and store in a cool, dark place. It will keep for 3–4 months.

A small amount of muscovado sugar gives this marmalade a good, rich flavour. For a tangy marmalade, use Seville oranges when they are in season.

three-fruit processor marmalade

makes: 2.25 kg (5 lb)
preparation time: 30 minutes, plus straining and standing
cooking time: about 1¼ hours

4 oranges
3 limes
2 lemons
1.5 litres (2½ pints) water
1.5 kg (3 lb) preserving or granulated sugar

If you would like to make marmalade, but are a little short of time, then this speedy fine-shred version uses a food processor to cut down on preparation time.

1 Thinly peel the rinds from the fruit, leaving the white pith behind. Put the rinds into a food processor and chop finely, then tip out on to a plate and reserve.

2 Quarter the fruits and process in two batches until roughly chopped. Place in a large pan with the water. Cover the pan and bring to the boil, then reduce the heat and simmer for 45 minutes until the pith is soft.

3 Pour the mixture through a fine sieve into a bowl and leave to drip for 30 minutes. Press out any remaining juice from the pith with the back of a spoon, then pour the juice back into the pan and add the chopped fruit rinds. Cover and simmer gently for 15 minutes until tender. Meanwhile, pour the sugar into a roasting tin and warm in a low oven (see page 7) for 10 minutes.

4 Add the warmed sugar to the pan and cook over a low heat, stirring continuously, until the sugar has completely dissolved. Increase the heat, bring to the boil and boil, uncovered, for 10–15 minutes, testing at 5-minute intervals until a set is reached. Using a slotted spoon, carefully skim off any scum, then leave the marmalade to stand for 15 minutes to allow the fruit to settle.

5 Stir well, then transfer to warm dry jars. Cover the surface of each with a disc of waxed paper, waxed side down, then leave until cold. Top the cold jars with airtight lids or cellophane covers. Label and store in a cool, dark place. It will keep for 6–12 months.

lime marmalade

makes: about 2.25 kg (5 lb)
preparation time: 30 minutes,
plus standing
cooking time: 2¼ hours

6 limes, washed, dried and
quartered lengthways
2 lemons, washed, dried and
quartered lengthways
1.5 litres (2½ pints) water
1.5 kg (3 lb) sugar

1 Cut the lime quarters into long, very fine slices, removing all the pips. Cut the lemon quarters in the same way and mix both fruits in a large pan. Pour in the water and bring to the boil, then reduce the heat and cover the pan. Simmer for 1½ hours.

2 Add the sugar to the pan and cook over a low heat, stirring continuously, until the sugar has completely dissolved. Increase the heat and bring to the boil, then boil hard to setting point. Using a slotted spoon, carefully skim off any scum, then leave the marmalade to stand for 15 minutes to allow the fruit to settle.

3 Stir well, then transfer to warm dry jars. Cover the surface of each with a disc of waxed paper, waxed side down, then leave until cold. Top the cold jars with airtight lids or cellophane covers. Label and store in a cool, dark place. It will keep for 3–4 months.

This is a delicious, flavoursome and slightly tangy marmalade. Although limes are sometimes quite expensive, this recipe gives a high yield, which compensates for the initial cost of the fruit.

spiced cranberry mincemeat with port

makes: 1.6 kg (3¼ lb)
preparation time: 20 minutes,
plus standing
cooking time: 5 minutes

250 g (8 oz) cranberries
1 large cooking apple, about
375 g (12 oz), peeled,
cored and diced
500 g (1 lb) bag luxury
mixed dried fruit
1 teaspoon ground cinnamon
½ teaspoon freshly
grated nutmeg
¼ teaspoon ground cloves
200 g (7 oz) soft light
brown sugar
125 g (4 oz) vegetable suet
grated rind of 1 orange
125 ml (4 fl oz) ruby port

*This chunky, luxury mincemeat
captures all the very best
Christmas aromas in a jar.
Spoon into pastry cases for truly
memorable mince pies and tarts.*

1 Put the cranberries and apple into a pan with 3 tablespoons of water and cook, uncovered, for 5 minutes, stirring occasionally, until the fruits are softened but still holding their shape. Leave to cool in the pan.

2 Put the dried fruit into a large bowl and mix in the remaining ingredients. Stir in the cooled cooked fruit, then cover the bowl and leave to stand overnight.

3 Stir the mincemeat mixture again, then spoon into warm dry jars. Cover the surface of each with a disc of waxed paper, waxed side down, then top with an airtight lid. Label and leave to mature in a cool, dark place for 3–4 weeks before using, or store, unopened, for up to 6 months.

tip If you prefer a more traditional 'minced meat' texture either put the dried fruits through a mincer or chop them in a food processor.

apricot & ginger mincemeat

makes: about 2 kg (4 lb)
preparation time: 30 minutes,
plus standing

50 g (2 oz) crystallized ginger
250 g (8 oz) dried apricots
250 g (8 oz) raisins
175 g (6 oz) sultanas
175 g (6 oz) currants
50 g (2 oz) chopped mixed peel
50 g (2 oz) blanched
almonds, chopped
250 g (8 oz) cooking apples,
peeled, cored and grated
juice and grated rind of
3 oranges
juice and grated rind of
2 lemons
250 g (8 oz) soft light
brown sugar
375 g (12 oz) carrots,
peeled and grated
¼ teaspoon freshly
grated nutmeg
½ teaspoon ground mixed spice
150 ml (¼ pint) brandy
4 tablespoons rum

1 Finely chop ginger, apricots, raisins and sultanas. Put them into a large bowl with the currants, mixed peel and almonds.

2 Put the apples into a separate bowl and mix in the orange and lemon rinds and juices, then stir into the chopped fruit with the sugar.

3 Next, add the carrots to the bowl with the spices, brandy and rum, then cover the bowl and leave the mincemeat to stand for 2 days, stirring it frequently.

4 Transfer the mincemeat to clean dry jars and cover the surface of each with a disc of waxed paper, waxed side down, then top with an airtight lid. Label and leave to mature in a cool, dark place for 3–4 weeks before using, or store, unopened, for up to 6 months.

Dried apricots and crystallized ginger make a deliciously unusual mincemeat. Try this recipe as an alternative to traditional mincemeat when making mince pies for Christmas.

blueberries in kirsch

makes: 400 g (13 oz)
preparation time: 10 minutes,
plus standing

175 g (6 oz) blueberries,
destalked
50 g (2 oz) caster sugar
100 ml (3½ fl oz) kirsch

1 Pick over the blueberries, discarding any very soft ones. Prick each berry with a fork, then layer in a clean dry jar, sprinkling each layer with some sugar.

2 Pour over the kirsch. Seal tightly and shake once or twice.

3 Leave in a cool place and turn the jar upside down every day for 4 days until the sugar has completely dissolved. Label and leave to mature in a cool, dark place for 3–4 weeks before using, or store, unopened, for 6–12 months.

Variation
You can also make this with fresh red or black pitted cherries.

Quick and simple to prepare yet deliciously indulgent to eat spooned over vanilla ice cream or pancakes and crème fraîche; or fold into whipped cream for a special cake filling.

figs in vanilla syrup

makes: 500 g (1 lb)
preparation time: 20 minutes
cooking time: 35–40 minutes

8–9 firm fresh figs, halved
100 g (4 oz) caster sugar
400 ml (7 fl oz) water
½ vanilla pod, slit lengthways
½ teaspoon citric acid

*Fresh figs are in season for only
a short time and, unlike many
summer fruits, do not freeze well
when baked in tarts or pies.
Capture their full flavour by
bottling in a rich vanilla syrup.*

1 Pack the figs with the cut sides facing the outside of a warm jar. Pack the centre of the jar tightly and put two halves, cut side uppermost, in the top of the jar.

2 Put the sugar, water and vanilla pod into a pan. Stirring continuously, slowly bring to the boil and heat until the sugar has completely dissolved. Boil for 1 minute, then remove from the heat.

3 Lift the vanilla pod out of the syrup and, using a small knife, scrape out the black seeds into the syrup and stir in the citric acid. Tuck the vanilla pod down the side of the jar.

4 Pour the syrup over the figs to cover completely and come almost to the brim of the jar. Top up with boiling water if needed and seal the jar. Stand the jar on a baking sheet lined with several sheets of folded newspaper and bake in a preheated oven, 150°C (300°F), Gas 2, for 40 minutes until the syrup has turned a delicate pink and the figs are just beginning to rise in the jar.

5 Using oven gloves, transfer the jar to a wooden board, close the clasp fully and leave to cool completely. When cold, check the jar seals (see page 9). Label and store in a cool, dark place. The figs will keep for 6–12 months.

green tomato chutney

makes: about 2 kg (4 lb)
preparation time: 15 minutes
cooking time: 1 hour
40 minutes

1 kg (2 lb) green tomatoes,
finely chopped
500 g (1 lb) onions,
finely chopped
500 g (1 lb) cooking apples,
peeled, cored and chopped
2 fresh green chillies, halved,
deseeded and finely chopped
2 garlic cloves, crushed
1 teaspoon ground ginger
generous pinch of ground
cloves
generous pinch of ground
turmeric
50 g (2 oz) raisins
250 g (8 oz) soft dark
brown sugar
300 ml (½ pint) white
wine vinegar

1 Put the tomatoes, onions, apples and chillies into a large pan and mix together. Add the garlic, ginger, cloves and turmeric, then stir in the raisins, sugar and vinegar.

2 Bring to the boil, reduce the heat and cover the pan. Simmer, stirring frequently, for 1¼–1½ hours or until the chutney has thickened.

3 Transfer the chutney to warm dry jars and cover the surface of each with a disc of waxed paper, waxed side down, then top with an airtight lid. Label and leave to mature in a cool, dark place for at least 3 weeks before using, or store, unopened, for 6–12 months.

If you grow tomatoes you will probably be left with some unripened fruit at the end of the season. But don't throw your green tomatoes away: chop them up and make a tempting chutney.

peach & date chutney

makes: 1.5–2 kg (3–4 lb)
preparation time: 10 minutes
cooking time: 50 minutes

12 peaches
500 g (1 lb) onions
2 garlic cloves, crushed
2 tablespoons grated
fresh root ginger
125 g (4 oz) pitted dates,
chopped
250 g (8 oz) demerara sugar
300 ml (½ pint) red
wine vinegar
salt and freshly ground
black pepper

1 Put the peaches into a large bowl, cover them with boiling water and leave to stand for about 1 minute, then drain and peel them. Halve and stone the fruit and cut it into thick slices.

2 Put the onions into a pan with the peaches, garlic, ginger, dates, sugar and vinegar. Add a generous sprinkling of salt and pepper and bring the mixture to the boil, stirring continuously, until the sugar has completely dissolved.

3 Reduce the heat, cover the pan and simmer, stirring frequently, for 45 minutes, until the chutney has thickened.

4 Transfer the chutney to warm dry jars. Cover the surface of each with a disc of waxed paper, waxed side down, then top with an airtight lid. Label and leave to mature in a cool, dark place for 2 weeks before using, or store, unopened, for 6–12 months.

The delicate flavour of the peaches makes this a good accompaniment to ripe, creamy Brie, full-fat soft cheeses and roast poultry. Perfect for serving with your cold roast Christmas turkey.

chestnut, red onion & fennel chutney

makes: about 625 g (1¼ lb)
preparation time: 15 minutes
cooking time: 1½ hours

60 ml (2½ fl oz) olive oil
4 large red onions, thinly sliced
1 fennel bulb, trimmed and
thinly sliced
250 g (8 oz) cooked, peeled
chestnuts, halved
100 g (3½ oz) soft light
brown sugar
125 ml (4 fl oz) cider vinegar
125 ml (4 fl oz) sweet sherry
or marsala wine
freshly ground black pepper

1 Heat the oil in a large pan, add the onions and fennel and cook gently for 25–30 minutes, until the onions are very soft.

2 Add the chestnuts, sugar, vinegar and sherry to the pan, season well with pepper and stir. Simmer gently, uncovered, stirring occasionally, for about 1 hour, until the chutney has thickened.

3 Transfer the chutney to a warm dry jar and cover the surface with a disc of waxed paper, waxed side down, then top with an airtight lid. Label and leave to cool completely before serving. Store in a cool, dark place or in the refrigerator. It will keep for 3–4 months.

This chutney is quick and easy to prepare and is the perfect partner to blue cheese, bread and cold meats for a quick and delicious lunch.

chilli & garlic chutney

makes: 750 g–1 kg (1½–2 lb)
preparation time: 15 minutes
cooking time: 30 minutes

500 g (1 lb) fresh chillies,
red or green
6 garlic cloves, crushed
4 tablespoons ground cumin
2 tablespoons ground
turmeric
1 large onion, finely chopped
1 tablespoon salt
25 g (1 oz) fresh root ginger,
grated
300 ml (½ pint)
groundnut oil
3 tablespoons muscovado
sugar
300 ml (½ pint) white
wine vinegar

1 Remove the stalks from the chillies then chop the chillies very finely, seeds and all.

2 Mix the chillies, garlic, cumin, turmeric, onion, salt, ginger and oil in a pan and fry for 15 minutes, stirring frequently. Add the sugar and vinegar and bring the mixture to the boil, then cover the pan and boil the chutney for 10 minutes, stirring occasionally.

3 Transfer the chutney to hot dry jars and cover the surface of each with a disc of waxed paper, waxed side down, then top with an airtight lid. Label and leave to cool completely before serving. Store in a cool, dark place or in the refrigerator. It will keep for up to 12 months. Stir the chutney well before using as the oil will separate out on standing.

Be warned – this spicy chutney is very hot. Serve with curries or mix a little with natural yogurt and spread the mixture over meat or poultry before cooking to make an exciting marinade.

piccalilli

makes: about 1 kg (2 lb)
preparation time: 10 minutes, plus standing
cooking time: 25 minutes

1 small cauliflower, broken into small florets, large stalks discarded
½ cucumber, thinly peeled and roughly chopped
2 onions, chopped
2 large carrots, peeled and cut into chunks
about 50 g (2 oz) salt
2 tablespoons plain flour
300 ml (½ pint) cider vinegar
250 g (8 oz) sugar
½ teaspoon ground turmeric
½ teaspoon ground ginger
2 teaspoons mustard powder
freshly ground black pepper

1 Layer the vegetables in a large bowl, sprinkling each layer with salt, then cover and leave to stand overnight. The next day, lightly rinse and thoroughly dry them.

2 Mix the flour to a smooth cream with a little of the vinegar. Heat the remaining vinegar in a large pan with the sugar, spices and mustard over a low heat, stirring continuously, until the sugar has dissolved. Increase the heat and bring to the boil, then season the mixture generously with pepper and add the vegetables. Bring back to the boil, then reduce the heat and simmer, uncovered, for 10 minutes.

3 Remove the pan from the heat and gradually stir in the flour mixture. Return to the heat, bring to the boil and simmer for a further 5 minutes. Transfer the pickle to warm dry jars and top with airtight lids. Label and leave to cool completely before serving. Store in a cool, dark place or in the refrigerator. It will keep for 6–9 months.

This pickle is traditionally very spicy with a crunchy texture. It is usually served with cold meats such as ham or roast pork, but can also do a wonderful job of spicing up a cheese sandwich.

marrow & onion pickle

makes: about 2.75 kg (6 lb)
preparation time: 30 minutes, plus standing
cooking time: 1¾ hours

1 medium marrow, about 2 kg (4 lb), peeled, halved lengthways and seeded
1 kg (2 lb) small pickling onions, halved
1 green or red pepper
250 g (8 oz) pitted dates
1 tablespoon freshly grated root ginger
600 ml (1 pint) spiced vinegar (see page 63)
500 g (1 lb) demerara sugar
salt

This is a chunky, sweet pickle, which tastes good with boiled or baked ham, roast meats and continental sausages.

1 Cut the marrow flesh into chunks and layer with the onions in a large bowl, salting each layer, then cover the bowl and leave overnight. The next day, lightly rinse and thoroughly dry the vegetables.

2 Put the salted vegetables into a large pan. Trim and deseed the pepper, remove the pith and chop the flesh finely. Chop the dates finely. Add these ingredients to the pan with the ginger, vinegar and sugar. Bring the mixture to the boil, stirring well to mix the ingredients. Reduce the heat, cover the pan and simmer, stirring frequently, for 1½ hours, until the mixture has thickened.

3 Transfer the pickle to warm dry jars and top with airtight lids. Label and leave to mature in a cool, dark place for 2 weeks before using, or store, unopened, for about 6 months.

lime pickle

makes: 500 g (1 lb)
preparation time: 10 minutes
cooking time: 5 minutes

10 limes, each cut into 6 sections
125 g (4 oz) sea salt
1 tablespoon fenugreek seeds
1 tablespoon black mustard seeds
1 tablespoon chilli powder
1 tablespoon ground turmeric
300 ml (½ pint) vegetable oil
½ teaspoon ground asafoetida

1 Put the limes into a large jar and cover with the salt.

2 Dry-fry the fenugreek and mustard seeds in a small nonstick frying pan, then grind them to a powder in either a mortar with a pestle, a spice grinder or a coffee grinder kept specially for the purpose.

3 Add the ground seeds, chilli powder and turmeric to the limes and mix well.

4 Heat the oil in a small frying pan until smoking, add the asafoetida and fry for 30 seconds. Pour the oil over the limes and mix well.

5 Cover the jar with a clean cloth and leave to mature for 10 days in a bright, warm place. Top with an airtight lid. Label and store in a cool, dark place. It will keep for 2 months.

This spicy pickle is served as an accompaniment to many Indian dishes but is also wonderful served just with rice, yogurt and a simple dhal.

beetroot & apple relish

makes: about 1.5 kg (3 lb)
preparation time: 15 minutes
cooking time: 1¾ hours

500 g (1 lb) cooking apples,
peeled, halved and cored
500 g (1 lb) raw beetroot,
peeled
375 g (12 oz) onions,
finely chopped
1 tablespoon finely chopped
fresh root ginger
2 large garlic cloves, crushed
1 teaspoon paprika
1 teaspoon ground turmeric
1 cinnamon stick
250 g (8 oz) soft dark
brown sugar
450 ml (¾ pint) red
wine vinegar

1 Grate the apples and beetroot into a large pan, then add all the remaining ingredients.

2 Bring the mixture to the boil, then reduce the heat and cover the pan. Simmer, stirring occasionally, for about 1½ hours, until the relish has thickened and the beetroot is tender.

3 Transfer the relish to warm dry jars and top with airtight lids. Label and leave to mature in a cool, dark place for about 1 week before using, or store, unopened, for 6–9 months.

Relishes, as their name suggests, are spicy and particularly suitable for serving with grills and barbecues. The beetroot in this recipe gives this relish a wonderful fresh taste.

sweetcorn relish

makes: about 1.5 kg (3 lb)
preparation time: 15 minutes
cooking time: 30 minutes

4 tablespoons corn oil
2 large onions, finely chopped
1 green pepper, cored,
deseeded and finely chopped
1 red pepper, cored, deseeded
and finely chopped
4 celery sticks, finely chopped
1 teaspoon salt
1 large garlic clove, crushed
2 carrots, peeled and cut into
small cubes
50 g (2 oz) sugar
2 teaspoons mustard powder
750 g (1½ lb) frozen
sweetcorn
450 ml (¾ pint) vinegar

1 Heat the oil in a large pan and add the onions, peppers and celery. Fry them until they are soft but not browned, then add the salt and garlic.

2 Add all the remaining ingredients to the pan and bring the mixture to the boil. Reduce the heat and cook, uncovered, for 15 minutes, stirring occasionally.

3 Transfer the relish to warm dry jars, pressing the vegetables well down into the juices, then top with airtight lids and leave to cool.

4 This relish does not need time to mature, but if not immediately consumed, label and store in a cool, dark place for 6 months.

No selection of pickles and relishes would be complete without American corn relish. Traditionally served with hamburgers, it is also wonderful with pizzas, cottage pie, cold roast meats and cheese.

white mustard with fine herbs

makes: 425 g (14 oz)
preparation time: 15 minutes,
plus standing

100 g (3½ oz) white
mustard seeds
75 g (3 oz) soft light brown sugar
1 teaspoon rock salt
1 teaspoon white peppercorns
½ teaspoon ground turmeric
275 ml (9 fl oz) white
wine vinegar
6 tablespoons chopped fresh
herbs to include rosemary,
sage, parsley, chives

1 Put all the dry ingredients into a food processor or blender and blend until the seeds are finely ground.

2 Gradually pour in the vinegar and blend until well mixed. Add the herbs and mix briefly.

3 Leave the mustard to stand for 1 hour to thicken, then transfer to warm dry jars. Cover the surface of each with a disc of waxed paper, waxed side down, then leave until cold. Top the cold jars with airtight lids or cellophane covers. Label and store in a cool, dark place. It will keep for 3–6 months.

Variation
If you would prefer to use just one type of herb, then reduce the total amount to 3 tablespoons.

Attractively flecked with fresh herbs, this mustard is delicious added to salad dressings. It can also be added to meaty sauces or served on its own with cold meats.

herby pickled plums

makes: 2 kg (4 lb)
preparation time: 20 minutes
cooking time: 2–2½ hours

750 ml (1¼ pints) white wine vinegar
500 g (1 lb) caster sugar
7 rosemary sprigs
7 thyme sprigs
7 small bay leaves
4 lavender sprigs (optional)
4 garlic cloves, unpeeled
1 teaspoon salt
½ teaspoon multi-coloured peppercorns
1.5 kg (3 lb) firm red plums, washed and pricked

Pickled plums are delicious served with cold meats, salad and a jacket potato. They also make an ideal present if a few extra herbs are tied decoratively on the clip of the jar with ribbon or raffia.

1 Use a standard slow cooker and preheat if necessary. Pour the vinegar and sugar into the cooker pot and add 4 each of the rosemary and thyme sprigs and bay leaves, all the lavender, if using, the garlic, salt and peppercorns. Cook on 'High' for 2–2½ hours, stirring once or twice.

2 Warm the clean jars in the bottom of a low oven. Pack the plums tightly into the warm dry jars and tuck the remaining fresh herbs into them. Strain in the hot vinegar, making sure that the plums are completely covered, then top with airtight lids.

3 Label and leave to mature in a cool, dark place for 3–4 weeks before using, or store, unopened, for 6–12 months. The plums will lose colour slightly.

Variation
Add a tiny dried chilli to each jar of plums or use some broken cinnamon sticks, juniper berries and pared orange rind in place of the fresh herbs.

pickled walnuts

makes: about 2 litres (3 pints)
preparation time: 10 minutes,
plus soaking and standing
cooking time: 15 minutes

500 g (1 lb) young fresh
walnuts
50 g (2 oz) salt
600 ml (1 pint) water
3 level teaspoons mixed
pickling spice
1.7 litres (3 pints) white
wine vinegar

*Use only young walnuts for this
recipe; if they are over-ripe they
will not pickle. Serve with both
cold meats and most varieties
of cheese – the textures of ripe
Brie or Camembert are very
complementary.*

1 Using a silver fork, prick each walnut deeply in 2 or 3 places.

2 To make the brine, add the salt to the water and stir to mix. Add the walnuts, ensuring they are covered in the brine, place a plate on top to keep them submerged and soak them for 14 days.

3 Remove the walnuts from the brine and place on a tray or cloth in the sun, shaking them occasionally. They will turn black after 2 or 3 days, or in 24 hours if it is very hot.

4 Meanwhile, make the spiced vinegar. Put the mixed pickling spice and vinegar into a pan and boil for 15 minutes. Strain and leave until cold.

5 When the walnuts are quite black, pack into jars and cover with the spiced vinegar. Top with airtight lids. Label and leave to mature in a cool, dark place for at least 1 month before using, or store, unopened, for 3–4 months.

index

Photography © Octopus
Publishing Group/
Stephen Conroy